MATT CHRISTOPHER

On the Court with...

MATT CHRISTOPHER

On the Court with...
Kobe Bryant

Text by Glenn Stout

Little, Brown and Company
Boston   New York   London

First Edition

Matt Christopher™ is a trademark of Catherine M. Christopher.

Cover photograph by E. J. Flynn

Library of Congress Cataloging-in-Publication Data

Stout, Glenn.
    On the court with . . . Kobe Bryant / text by Glenn Stout. — 1st ed.
       p.   cm.
    ISBN 0-316-13732-4
    1. Bryant, Kobe, 1978– — Juvenile literature. 2. Basketball players — United States — Biography — Juvenile literature. [1. Bryant, Kobe, 1978– 2. Basketball players. 3. Afro-Americans — Biography.] I. Title: At head of title: Matt Christopher. II. Christopher, Matt. III. Title.
GV884.B794 S76   2001
796.323'092 — dc21
[B]   00-050092

10 9 8 7 6 5 4 3 2

COM-MO

Printed in the United States of America

Contents

MATT CHRISTOPHER

On the Court with...

Chapter One:

1978–1983

Jellybean Goes to Italy

If you look in the 1983–1984 edition of the *Official National Basketball Association Register,* you can find the complete career statistics of Joe "Jellybean" Bryant.

Nothing in the record of the six-foot-nine-and-one-half-inch, 215-pound center-forward really stands out. It states that he graduated from John Bartram High School in Philadelphia and attended LaSalle College for three years, averaging just over 20 points per game in two seasons of basketball. In 1976 he left school and was selected in the first round of the NBA draft.

From 1976 to 1983, Jellybean, who earned his nickname after some young fans gave him jellybeans following a game, played with the Philadelphia 76ers, San Diego Clippers, and Houston Rockets.

He had a solid career in the NBA, averaging eight points a game and earning a reputation as a fine passer and a defensive specialist. But Bryant wasn't quite big enough to play center full-time and didn't shoot quite well enough to play forward. He was wonderfully athletic, but in some ways was ahead of his time, for his flashy style of play wasn't much appreciated in the NBA two decades ago. He was a role player who left the spotlight to teammates like future Hall-of-Famers Elvin Hayes and Julius Erving. None of his teams ever won an NBA championship, and Bryant never made an All-Star team.

Yet none of that begins to measure Joe Bryant's contribution to the NBA. For in the long run, Joe Bryant may have left a greater legacy to the NBA than many of its better-known stars.

That's because Joe Bryant is the father of the Los Angeles Lakers' Kobe Bryant, one of the youngest and brightest stars in the NBA, a player who joined the NBA directly out of high school. The son's career has already eclipsed that of the father. Kobe Bryant has already been an All-Star, won the NBA Slam Dunk Contest, and won an NBA championship. His story began when his father's NBA career came to an end.

After the 1982–83 NBA season, Joe Bryant's career was at a crossroads. After eight seasons in the NBA, including three years as a starter for the Houston Rockets, Bryant had become a second-string player. He had settled into a backup role on the Rockets, who had finished with a record of 14–68, the worst in the league.

That finish gave them the right to select seven-foot-four-inch center Ralph Sampson, the best player in college basketball, in the NBA draft. That may have been good news for Rocket fans, but it wasn't very good news for Joe Bryant. Now that they had Sampson, the Rockets didn't really need Bryant. So, at the end of the season, the Rockets released him.

No other team in the NBA expressed much interest in signing the veteran, preferring to stock their rosters with younger and cheaper players. At age twenty-eight, it appeared as if Joe's career as a professional basketball player had come to an end.

The popular Bryant probably could have gone

into business in Houston, but he and his wife, Pam, also a Philadelphia native, decided to return home.

Bryant quickly discovered that he missed the game of basketball. But he didn't want to coach or anything like that. He still wanted to play.

Fortunately, Bryant was a good friend of a man named Sonny Hill. Hill ran a well-known summer league in Philadelphia and had contacts throughout the basketball world. He told Bryant about a unique opportunity to keep playing the game he loved.

Although basketball had been invented in the United States, the game had spread all over the globe and was probably the world's second most popular sport, after soccer. Several European countries even supported their own professional leagues.

Like all pro sports leagues, they were always on the lookout for talent. And the United States was still the home of the best basketball players in the world. Representatives of the Italian professional league had contacted Hill and told him they were in the market for some talented American players. They paid well and played a much shorter, easier schedule than the NBA, usually with only one game a week. Hill told Bryant he should consider playing in Italy. When Bryant said he was interested, Hill put him in touch with the Italians.

Bryant was precisely the kind of player the Italians wanted. His NBA background, size, and skills were guaranteed to make him a star in the Italian league. Moreover, his effervescent personality was certain to make him a crowd favorite. Bryant was intrigued, and not just because it meant he could keep playing basketball.

When Joe had played in the NBA, he'd spent a lot of time on the road. He sometimes went a week or more without seeing his family. Joe and Pam were the parents of three young children. Their oldest daughter, Sharia, was seven years old, sister Shaya was six, and Kobe, named after a city in Japan and born on August 23, 1978, was five. While Bryant still held out some hope of returning to the NBA, he worried about the effect such continued absences would have on his family.

The more Joe and Pam discussed the possibility of moving to Italy, the better it sounded. The money was good and the lighter schedule meant he'd be able to spend a great deal of time with his family. In addition, they thought that living in Italy and traveling around Europe would be a wonderful opportunity for their children to experience a different culture. They decided to accept the offer and move to Italy.

Kobe Bryant's basketball education was ready to begin.

Chapter Two:
1984-1991

His Father's Son

The Bryants packed up their belongings and moved to Rieti, Italy, in 1984. While Joe Bryant was learning the ins and outs of Italian basketball and Pam Bryant was finding her way around a new city, Sharia, Shaya, and Kobe, who had just turned six, started attending an Italian school.

Surprisingly, the Bryants' three children had a relatively easy time adjusting to their new culture. Children are adept at learning new languages. Although they didn't understand a word of Italian when they began school, as Kobe later explained, "My two sisters and I got together after school to teach each other the words we had learned. I was able to speak Italian pretty well within a few months."

Joe Bryant experienced a similarly quick transition

to basketball Italian-style. On his Italian team, he was the "go-to" guy, the player who was supposed to score points and entertain the fans. He thrived in the somewhat less-competitive league. Few players could match his blend of size and quickness. He averaged over 30 points per game and wowed the crowd with dunks, long jumpers, and no-look passes. In a matter of weeks, he became one of the league's best-known and most popular stars. The fans even made up songs about him claiming he was a better player than NBA stars like Kareem Abdul-Jabbar.

The family loved their new life. They enjoyed traveling around Europe to see such sights as the Roman Collosseum in Italy and the Eiffel Tower in Paris. They also enjoyed the opportunity to experience new cultures. In much of Europe, for example, people don't buy all their food at grocery stores. Instead, they often shop at outdoor markets full of fresh fruits and vegetables. But for the Bryants, the best part of living in Europe was the fact that the entire family got to spend so much time together.

Although they faced little prejudice in Europe because of their African-American heritage, it was still difficult, particularly at first, for them to make friends. So they turned to each other for strength and company.

Kobe loved being around his father. He went to many of his games and loved seeing the way the crowd reacted to his father's spectacular play. He often played basketball with his father and his sisters, and at six years old could already dribble and shoot.

Kobe's grandparents were always sending the family packages filled with videotapes of American television and movies that were impossible to see in Italy. Usually, they included a large number of tapes of the NBA, which at that time was only rarely broadcast in Europe.

Kobe loved sitting with his father and watching the tapes of games. As they watched, Joe analyzed the play and explained what was happening on the court to Kobe. It was as if Kobe was attending his own private basketball school.

Of all the players Kobe watched on the tapes, his absolute favorite was guard Earvin "Magic" Johnson of the Los Angeles Lakers. The six-foot-nine Johnson led the champion Lakers, and his unique combination of skills took the game into a new era. For despite his size, Johnson played point guard and proved that skilled taller players can be just as adept at guard play as smaller men. Kobe watched the tapes of Johnson over and over again, and put pictures of the Lakers' star all over his room.

Kobe's fascination with Johnson continued even when he was playing. But although there was a basketball court at Kobe's school, he had a hard time finding other kids who wanted to play. Unfortunately for Kobe, most Italian children preferred to play soccer.

While Kobe learned to play soccer and enjoyed the game, basketball was his favorite sport. So when he couldn't talk other children into playing basketball, he played by himself.

He invented a game he called "shadow basketball," telling people later that he "played against [his] shadow." What Kobe meant was that while playing alone he learned to imagine a court full of players and played entire games against imaginary opponents. Sometimes he'd pretend he was Magic Johnson leading the Lakers' fast break, and other times he'd pretend he was his father. His ability to visualize basketball situations and then react to them would later prove invaluable to his development as a player. In fact, Kobe still plays shadow basketball today.

But shadow basketball still wasn't like playing on a team. So Joe had Kobe join a club team.

In most of Europe, organized sports are run by clubs. A single basketball club, for instance, sponsors a number of teams ranging from youth teams to teams of adults. Since basketball isn't a sport most Italians play while growing up, the focus is on fundamentals.

As a result, when Kobe was learning the game he spent untold hours doing drills, learning the correct way to dribble, shoot, and guard his opponent. In contrast, most American youngsters learn the game on the playground, where it is easy to pick up bad habits.

But since Kobe learned how to play the right way from the very beginning, he didn't have any bad habits. Playing club basketball, combined with watching his father and tapes of the NBA, gave him a sound foundation in the sport. Kobe never developed any bad habits that he had to break. From the time he was a child, his game was fundamentally sound.

Meanwhile, Joe Bryant was in an enviable position.

He was one of the best and most popular players in Europe. Every time his contract was up, a number of teams would clamor for his services.

He switched teams several times, causing his family to move. But they didn't mind. Being together was all that mattered.

Every year they went back to Philadelphia to visit with family. Kobe loved going back to see his grandparents, and he also enjoyed the opportunity to play pickup basketball with neighborhood kids. And even though they would be in America only a few weeks, his father would sign him up for the local youth basketball league, the Sonny Hill League, so he could continue to improve and be exposed to a different style of play.

When Kobe was eleven years old, he began to grow taller. Over the course of the next two years he grew more than a foot, to over six feet tall. He towered above most of the other kids in school.

For many children, growing so fast can lead to a period of awkwardness as they adapt to their growing body. But Kobe was playing so much basketball that his coordination was able to keep pace with his growth. His game improved exponentially.

He was soon one of the best players on his club, regardless of age. He learned to dunk the basketball and could imitate many of the moves he had learned from watching the tapes and his father, and from playing shadow basketball. His friends would tease him, however, saying that while he was becoming a good European player, he "wouldn't be so good in America." Kobe tried to laugh it off, but he was beginning to suspect the same thing. He wanted to play in the NBA someday, just like his father had. But would he be good enough?

Joe Bryant had been paying close attention to how well Kobe was playing basketball. He was aware of his son's worries. He himself had now been playing professional basketball for sixteen seasons and he was beginning to slow down. In fact, when Kobe and Joe played one-on-one, Joe had to play hard in order to beat his son. While still a valuable player, he wasn't a big star anymore. Although he probably could have held on and kept playing for another year or two, he was financially secure. So, when Kobe was thirteen, Joe retired.

The Bryants decided that it was time to return to the United States. In the United States, Joe knew that Kobe could continue to work on his game, maybe earn a college scholarship, and, perhaps, play in the NBA. Those opportunities simply weren't available in Europe. His son needed better competition, and the entire family was ready to move on to another stage in their lives.

It was time for Kobe Bryant to go home.

Chapter Three:

1992

Back to America

Moving back to the United States after being away for eight years was far more difficult for Kobe than moving to Europe had been. He was older and was leaving all his friends behind. He had become comfortable living in Europe. Now, America was almost a foreign land to him.

Kobe had lived abroad for so long that he no longer spoke English very well. And many things that were familiar to most American kids, like the most popular TV shows and musical groups, were almost unknown to him. Kobe didn't have much in common with other American teenagers.

The Bryants moved to a suburb of Philadelphia, just outside the city limits. They enrolled Kobe in eighth grade at the local middle school.

At first, Kobe was overwhelmed. The school was

much different and much, much bigger than the school he had attended in Italy. Although Kobe was a very good student and soon discovered that in many ways his classes were easier than they had been in Italy, he struggled with the language and initially found it hard to make friends.

He was, quite literally, caught between two worlds. As he later remembered, "That made me the odd man out from the jump." The situation was made even worse by the fact that he was going through adolescence, an awkward stage of growing up that everyone goes through. Many adolescents lose confidence and don't feel very good about themselves as they struggle to make the transition from child to adult. Kobe had particular difficulty learning how to relate to other African Americans at his school. After all, when he was living in Italy about the only African-American faces he saw were those of his parents and two sisters. Kobe hadn't had any close African-American friends since he was a little kid.

The street slang used by many of his peers was particularly hard for Kobe to understand. "Blacks have their own way of talking," he recalled later, "and I really had to learn two languages in order to fit."

His situation wasn't helped by the fact that Kobe already stood well over six feet tall and towered over many of his peers. He often found himself the butt of their pranks and jokes.

But on his very first day of school Kobe discovered that he knew a universal language that could help break down the social barriers he faced. That language was the sport of basketball.

On that first day, as Kobe sat alone in the cafeteria eating his lunch, a classmate sauntered over and stood before him, sizing him up. When Kobe realized the other young man was staring at him, he slowly raised his eyes and looked up.

"I hear you're a pretty good basketball player," said his classmate with a sneer. Word had spread rapidly that the new student with the funny accent was the son of Joe Bryant, who was still well known in Philadelphia.

Kobe tried to stay cool. He wasn't quite sure what the other student was trying to say. He just looked the boy in the eye and slowly nodded.

"Well, to be the man you have to beat the man," said the student, gesturing to himself. Now Kobe noticed that several of the young man's friends hovered nearby, awaiting his reaction.

Kobe realized that if he acted as if he was intimidated, they might give him a hard time. He knew he was being challenged, but he also knew that if there was one thing he could do, it was play basketball.

"Okay," he said confidently, "let's play." Kobe and the other young man then made arrangements to play one-on-one after school.

Word quickly spread around the school that the new kid had accepted the challenge to play the best player in the school. When Kobe got to the court there were dozens of students ringing it to watch the matchup. His challenger was already warming up and bragging to his friends about how bad he was going to beat Kobe.

Kobe didn't quite understand the attitude of his opponent, for as he later admitted, "I didn't understand the school-yard rules, the trash-talking, the machismo." But he did understand basketball. He tried to ignore his opponent's boasting and called for the ball and started to play. The crowd buzzed with anticipation.

For the next twenty minutes or so Kobe and his challenger went at each other, but in a matter of only a few minutes the outcome was obvious. Every time his opponent got the ball, Kobe was all over him, blocking his drive, sticking a hand in his face, and swiping at the ball. The other player could hardly get a shot off. When he did, it either clanged off the rim or missed the rim entirely for an air ball.

When Kobe had the ball, it was another story. He discovered he was much quicker than his opponent was, had better footwork, could jump higher, and was far more skilled. For although his opponent was talented, he had learned to play on the playground and lacked the sound set of basketball fundamentals that Kobe had learned by playing on his club team in Italy, by himself, and with his father.

For example, when his opponent tried to guard him aggressively and bang him away from the basket, Kobe knew better than to try to force up a shot. Instead, he'd throw a fake, spin past him in a blur, and soar to the basket for an easy layup. When the player adjusted and backed off to prevent Kobe from driving past him, Kobe didn't try to bull his way to the hoop. Instead, he calmly drilled one jump shot after another.

The crowd soon quieted, then started cheering for Kobe as he poured the ball into the hoop over and over again. Then Kobe did something remarkable.

As his frustrated opponent came out to challenge him for the ball, Kobe faked left then drove to his right, soared through the air, and slammed the ball home.

The shocked crowd turned silent for a moment, then erupted in cheers. Kobe Bryant, an eighth-grader, had dunked the ball! As one of his friends said later, "I never saw a player like that. You just don't see guys in the eighth grade flying through the air and dunking the basketball."

A few minutes later, exhausted, his opponent gave up and the two young men shook hands. "I got my respect right there," Kobe remembers.

Although Kobe would still experience some awkward moments adjusting to his new school, he had taken an important first step. In addition to his family, basketball was the only other aspect of his life in Italy that was familiar to him in America. Even though he would occasionally have to struggle to make himself understood, he learned that basketball was a language that everyone knew.

Kobe soon found that he was welcome to play on the local playground and began making friends. At first the other players occasionally tried to test him and disrupt his game with trash talk and rough play. But Kobe quickly adjusted, not by adopting the same tactics, but by using his skills to render them ineffective. Kobe responded to trash talk by making his next shot, and he reacted to overly aggressive play by turning his game up a notch.

He also joined the eighth-grade team and quickly became the star, scoring at will. He was already looking forward to playing basketball at his local high school, Lower Merion. Their basketball team, the Aces, was one of the best teams in suburban Philadelphia and would soon finish the season with a stellar record of 20–5.

Aces coach Gregg Downer soon heard rumors about the eighth-grader. Curious about him, he invited Kobe to participate in one of the Aces' practices.

He figured that watching Kobe scrimmage against better, more experienced players would give him an idea of just how good Kobe was and what work he would have to do to play varsity basketball someday.

He saw a youthful, quiet, very thin thirteen-year-old amble into the gym. Nothing about the way he carried himself screamed that he was a basketball player.

He inserted Kobe into a scrimmage and sat back to watch. Within moments, he was stunned.

Kobe didn't just keep up with the varsity — he dominated them, getting off his shot with ease, stealing the ball, and rebounding. Downer's team included several players who had already won college scholarships. Yet Kobe already appeared to be the best player on the floor.

Unable to believe his eyes, Downer then asked Kobe to play him one-on-one. Downer himself had played college basketball and still played in a competitive adult league. He had to see for himself if Kobe was really that good.

He was. The coach went down to a quick defeat at the hands of the student.

Downer began to look forward to having Bryant

on his team. Four of the five starting players on the Aces were scheduled to graduate. Downer knew he would have to rebuild, and everyone was expecting Lower Merion to slip back in the pack. Despite their current record, the suburban school just didn't have the reputation of a basketball powerhouse.

Kobe wanted to be part of the rebuilding plan. His goal was not just to make the team, but to become a member of the starting lineup.

Very few freshmen make the varsity team in any high school sport. Most underclassmen have to play a season or two of junior varsity basketball against players of similar skill levels and experience before they can play effectively on the varsity. Basketball great Michael Jordan, for instance, was cut from his team as a freshman and didn't make the varsity until his junior year. Even fewer freshmen make the starting lineup.

But Kobe wasn't like most freshmen. He was more mature, both physically and mentally. By playing club basketball in Italy, with its focus on fundamentals and team play, he already knew how to play the game in a system. Most freshmen, despite the skills developed on the playground, have very little concept of team basketball. They have to learn to play an entirely new way.

Kobe worked out long and hard during the off-season, adding weight training to his regimen to become stronger. As the beginning of the basketball season approached, expectations for Kobe Bryant and the Aces were high. As the son of a former NBA player who had been one of the best basketball players ever to come out of the Philadelphia area, everyone expected Kobe to be an immediate star.

In practice, Coach Downer continued to be impressed. "He's a very talented player," he told the press at the beginning of the season. "He has the ability to do everything well."

But he was also cautious with his young star. "I'm not applying a lot of pressure on him," he insisted. To help with Kobe's transition, Downer even asked Joe Bryant to serve as an assistant coach.

Kobe, who sprouted to six-foot-four at age fourteen, easily earned a place in the starting lineup as a guard. Now all he had to do was play.

But by their opening game, it became clear that the 1992–93 season would be difficult for the Aces. Their two best returning players, center Matt Sniderland and guard Sultan Shabazz, were injured and wouldn't be able to play for the first month.

A tough schedule in the Central League, one of the best high school leagues in the state, didn't help. Time and time again the Aces stayed close only to lose in the final moments.

But Kobe was everything Downer had expected, and then some. He was often the best player on the floor, and always the youngest. Although there were times he could score at will, Downer was even more impressed by his court savvy and willingness to play in a team concept. When the opposition began double- and triple-teaming him, Bryant didn't force his shot. Instead, he looked to pass and involve his teammates in the game.

Although the Aces finished the season with a dismal 4–20 record, including 3–15 in league play, they played hard all season long and didn't give up. Bryant led the team in scoring, averaging 18 points per game, despite breaking his kneecap and missing the final few games of the season.

Kobe ended the season with a new goal. He told a friend that he wanted to play in the NBA.

That goal itself was no surprise, but when Kobe

planned to enter the NBA was. He told his friend he didn't want to go to college first. He wanted to go straight to the NBA from high school.

His friend just laughed. Only a handful of players had ever entered the NBA directly from high school. Even Michael Jordan hadn't been good enough to do that.

But Kobe was serious. He and his buddy made a friendly wager over Kobe's dream, which he kept a secret from his family.

But it wouldn't remain a secret for very much longer.

Chapter Four:
1993–1995

The Ace of the Aces

When his knee healed in the spring of 1993, Kobe immediately went back to work on his game. That meant playing against his father and his uncle, John "Chubby" Cox, who had briefly played in the NBA himself. The three spent hours on the driveway court at the Bryant home.

They worked on everything — free throw shooting, dribbling, driving to the basket, and shooting. When they played one-on-one, Kobe got a chance to try out his offensive skills on a player bigger and more experienced than he was. He also had to play tough defense in order to stop his father and uncle. The competition was much more intense than playing high school basketball.

As talented as Kobe was, Joe Bryant was six-foot-nine, experienced, still in shape, and still able to provide more than enough competition for his son. In their practice sessions, he played hard, knowing that Kobe wouldn't improve if he took it easy on him. By the end of the summer Kobe was occasionally beating his father.

One time that summer Kobe blasted by his father, soared to the hoop, and laid the ball in the basket. As he turned the ball back over to his father, a wry smile formed on Kobe's face. He knew he was improving and thought his father could no longer keep up with him.

Joe Bryant noted his son's growing confidence and decided to teach him a lesson. He dribbled the ball slowly and moved in toward the basket as his son guarded him, waving his hands in the air. Then Joe Bryant saw his chance. Overconfident, Kobe had overplayed him and was just a little out of position, with his weight on his heels.

That was the only advantage a player as good as Joe Bryant needed. He swirled around his son, jumped to the hoop, and stuffed a thunderous jam through the basket. Kobe was left behind, his feet still stuck to the ground.

He realized he still had a lot to work on. "I didn't think he was that quick," Kobe said later.

When basketball season started that fall, Kobe was much improved. He'd grown another inch and was even stronger and faster than he had been the previous season. And, like his teammates, he had the added benefit of a year of experience playing basketball at the varsity level.

Downer was impressed with the improvements in Kobe's game. "He does it all," he said. "He's a very complete ballplayer and at this time he's got the total package. He doesn't have a weakness." The coach told the press he expected his team to finish the year with a record above .500, a significant turnaround.

Kobe knew that Downer would expect even more of him in his sophomore season, but he had confidence in his game. "I don't think of it as pressure," he said of the expectations that everyone had for him. "I'm young and for me it's just fun and games. I think we'll be a lot better than four and twenty."

With Kobe leading the way, the Aces were much improved. They now won many of the close contests they had lost the previous season. Kobe upped his scoring average to 22 points and also averaged ten rebounds per game. The Aces went 16–6 and made it into the second round of the Pennsylvania Interscholastic Athletic Association's state basketball tournament.

After the season Kobe continued to work on his game. Basketball became a near full-time occupation, particularly in the summer. He played in no less than six different summer leagues, including the prestigious Sonny Hill League, whose alumni included many players, like Joe Bryant, who had become professionals. He also attended the LaSalle College basketball camp and the ABCD camp in New Jersey, which attracted some of the best high school basketball talent in the nation. Some days, he began playing at 9:00 A.M. and didn't stop until 9:30 at night. Of his grueling schedule, Kobe said, "I just love the game. I want to play as much as I can while I can. As long as I'm happy playing, I'll play all day and all night."

Eddie Jones, a star at Temple University who later excelled in the NBA, spotted Kobe in the Hill League and befriended him. He became his unofficial escort, taking him to inner-city Philadelphia to play against the best collegiate talent in the area. Kobe fit right in, as he had learned to add school-yard moves like the crossover dribble to his game. He was virtually unstoppable.

In his junior year at Lower Merion, everyone expected Kobe to lead the team to the league title and, possibly, the state championship. For although the Aces had lost three valuable seniors from the previous season, the remainder of the team now had the experience they had lacked in the past. As Downer said of his team, "We have plenty of talented kids besides [Bryant]. We'll be more than a one-player team."

The Aces got off to a fast start and at midseason were a stellar 11–1. Basketball fans throughout Philadelphia looked forward to their next game, which matched them with powerhouse Coatesville, one of the best teams in the state.

Coatesville had their own superstar in forward Richard Hamilton, a player many thought was even more talented than Kobe. He would later lead the University of Connecticut to an NCAA championship and play in the NBA.

The game was incredibly close. Kobe scored 16

points in the first half, but Coatesville still led at the half, 33–29. But entering the final quarter, Lower Merion nursed a one-point lead.

The teams traded the lead back and forth several times before Lower Merion pulled ahead by four points with less than a minute to play. But Coatesville didn't give up.

Trailing by two with only seconds left, Hamilton got the ball on the right side of the basket. He drove toward the hoop, then spun into the lane.

Kobe came out to stop him, but the wiry Hamilton twisted and ducked beneath him, rolling in a lay-up to send the game into overtime.

Again the clubs traded the lead back and forth. Then, while trying to guard Kobe, Hamilton fouled out of the game.

But Coatesville responded to the loss of their star and led, 77–73, with less than a minute to play. It looked like the Aces were going to fall short.

Kobe patiently dribbled the ball upcourt as Coatesville scrambled to set their defense. When he was twenty-five feet from the hoop, they backed off, covering the passing lanes and blocking his way to the basket.

Kobe didn't hesitate. He launched into the air and shot.

The ball soared in a high arc and then came down. *Swish!* The ball hit nothing but net and the referee threw up both his hands, signaling a three-point basket. Now Coatesville led by only one point.

Lower Merion needed to get the ball back and quickly fouled. When Coatesville missed the foul shot, Kobe swooped in and grabbed the rebound.

The crowd was roaring as Kobe dribbled downcourt and the clock ticked down. Ten . . . nine . . . eight . . .

As Kobe crossed midcourt , he picked up his pace, cutting first to the right and then to the left, past a defender just above the free throw line as he looked for an opening.

Seven . . . six . . . five . . .

He spotted an opening between defenders and slashed into the lane.

Four . . . three . . .

As several Coatesville defenders raised their arms and swarmed over him, Kobe pulled up, jumped, and shot a soft six-footer.

Two . . .

Swish! The ball found the bottom of the net! Kobe and the Aces won, 78–77!

The big win put the Aces in position to dethrone the defending Central League champions, Ridley High. In early February, the two teams met to decide the title.

The Aces trailed by five, 51–46, entering the fourth quarter. Then Kobe took over.

In the final period he poured in 13 points and set up forward Jermaine Griffin for several easy baskets for another 12. Lower Merion won going away, 76–70. Kobe described the game later. "It was like a heavyweight fight. We would not take no for an answer." Kobe finished with a career-high 42 points.

The win clinched the league title for the Aces, and they began to look ahead to the state tournament. But in their district quarterfinal versus Norristown, Kobe played poorly at first, missing several easy shots.

The vocal Norristown crowd took notice and began to taunt Kobe, chanting, "O-ver-ra-ted." It seemed to work at first, as Kobe couldn't get his game going. At halftime, Kobe had only six points and the Aces trailed by eight, 35–27.

But in the second half he responded to the pressure like the professional he wanted to be. He scored an incredible 29 second-half points, including 18 in the fourth period. Lower Merion fought back to win, 75–70. By the end of the game the only noise from the crowd came from delirious Lower Merion fans. "It's the best feeling in the world to silence an opposing crowd," said Kobe after the game.

The Aces fought their way into the state tournament, then ran up against a tough Hazelton team. Despite Kobe's 33 points and 15 rebounds, the Aces lost, 64–59, in overtime.

Kobe was crushed. After the game he broke down in tears and apologized to his teammates for not doing more in the loss.

His teammates and coach scoffed at his apology. As one teammate said later, "Playing with Kobe makes you play better." They all knew Kobe had done everything he could to help them win.

But Kobe Bryant was still determined to become even better. With only one year remaining in his high school career, he hadn't forgotten about his dream of playing in the NBA.

Chapter Five:
1995–1996

Senior Season

One of Bryant's classmates was the daughter of Philadelphia 76er coach John Lucas. One day in the summer before Kobe's senior year at Lower Merion, she told her father that he should see Kobe play. He did, and soon afterward invited Kobe to the gym at St. Joseph's College. When Kobe arrived, Lucas said, "I've got a surprise for you."

In walked 76er star Jerry Stackhouse. Lucas asked him to play Kobe one-on-one. In a few moments it became clear that Kobe could keep up with the NBA star. Afterward, Lucas asked Kobe if he'd like to work out with some of the other 76er players.

Although the 76ers didn't hold any official practices during the summer, some members of the team and other pros who lived in the Philadelphia area regularly got together at the college gym to scrimmage. Kobe jumped at Lucas's offer. It was another chance to play basketball and improve his skills.

Kobe was excited, but he wasn't nervous. Nothing about basketball made him nervous. "I had no butterflies," he said later. "No nothing. I never felt intimidated."

Few young players would have had the same response, for the group included players such as New Jersey Nets' tough guy Rich Mahorn and 76ers Dana Barros, Clarence Weatherspoon, and seven-foot-six-inch center Shawn Bradley, in addition to Stackhouse.

Although many of the pros were initially skeptical about playing with a high school student, Kobe soon won them over with his play. As Mahorn said later, "He blended with the rest of us," not the best player on the court, but not the worst, either. "He even tried to 'poster' [dunk] on me," recalled Mahorn. The burly big man rejected Bryant's shot, but offered, "That's not the point. He actually tried."

They would play for hours, competing in a series of games to eleven baskets, then choosing new sides and playing again. The games were more than a test of skill. They were also a test of stamina and desire.

Kobe proved he had all three. In one memorable contest, Kobe was matched up against the 76ers' Willie Burton, an explosive offensive player who had scored a team-best 53 points in a regular-season game the previous season.

The first time down the court, Burton took the ball to Kobe and popped in a jumper over his head. As they ran back upcourt, Burton threw some trash talk Kobe's way.

Kobe didn't get mad. He got even. On defense, Kobe hounded Burton the remainder of the game, limiting him to only one more basket. On offense, he showed the veteran that he had some skills of his own, scoring every way possible — hitting long jumpers, driving to the hoop, and dunking the ball. Kobe scored ten of his team's eleven baskets as they romped to a win.

Burton stormed off the court after the game and never returned to the 76ers. The last anyone heard, he was playing in Europe.

Kobe's performance caused him to revisit the wager he had made with his friend a few years before. "After a while," said Bryant of his experience playing with the pros, "it kind of popped into my mind that I can play with these guys. I could get to the hole, I could hit the jumper, I could score, although not at will, but I could get some shots. I was able to create for my teammates and rebound. Plus, the guys respected me, and when they respect you, that must mean something."

Before the summer was over, Kobe's confidence received several more boosts. At the prestigious ABCD camp, a showcase of high school talent, he was named MVP. At the Adidas Big Time Tournament, a similar event, he earned first-team honors. Then he added another MVP title playing in Pennsylvania's Keystone Games, scoring 47 points in the final to lead his Delaware Valley Team to the title over Philadelphia. Commented Gregg Downer afterward, "Kobe's just in a league of his own, really. He just has levels of his game that no high school player has possibly ever reached."

By the time Kobe returned to school to begin his senior year, virtually every top-notch college in the country was trying to convince him to accept a scholarship. Most scouting services were calling him the best high school player in the country. But he was also attractive to colleges for another reason.

Not only was he a great player, he was also a great student who carried a grade-point average above 3.0 and had scored well over 1,000 on his SAT, and important test required of most students considering college. Kobe had both the athletic and academic skills to succeed in college.

Some observers expected Kobe to attend nearby LaSalle, which was Joe Bryant's alma mater and where he now served as assistant basketball coach. Many thought that LaSalle had hired Bryant just to give them an edge in recruiting Kobe.

Joe Bryant scoffed at that charge, and also dismissed any notion that he was pressuring his son to attend LaSalle. Early that fall he told the press, "I'm a father first. If I couldn't look out for Kobe's best interest, I wouldn't have taken this job." Then he tipped off the press to another possibility. "What I tell Kobe is that he can go to any college that he wants to. Yet, then, Kobe's dream has always been to play in the NBA and that dream is more a reality for him now. If that's what he wants, why should he not go?"

The father and son had already discussed the topic, and as Kobe noted at the time, "My parents raised me to be an individual, to make my own decisions, and this is my decision." It wasn't a secret anymore that Kobe Bryant wanted to go straight to the NBA. His father had become convinced that Kobe could do so after he had seen the way Kobe had played against the pros that summer. He still knew many people who worked in the NBA and knew that word of Kobe's play had filtered up to pro scouts. They were beginning to look at him as closely as the colleges were.

But the possibility that Kobe Bryant might move directly from high school to the NBA was controversial. For many years, the NBA had not allowed its teams to sign high school players. When they finally changed the rule, only a handful successfully made the transition from high school to pro basketball. They had all been big men, like Moses Malone, Darryl Dawkins, and most recently, Minnesota Timberwolves star Kevin Garnett.

But some observers thought it would be irresponsible for Joe Bryant to allow his son to skip college. They believed Kobe wasn't mature enough for pro basketball or the pro lifestyle and warned that if he failed, or lost his confidence, his career could be ruined.

Some people also thought that Joe Bryant was

pressuring Kobe to play pro basketball to make up for his own disappointing NBA career. Bryant dismissed the notion. "I don't need to live my life through Kobe," he said. "I've already played in the NBA."

All those concerns would have been valid for most high school players, but Kobe was different. Growing up in Europe and around pro basketball for his entire life left him mature beyond his years. As Joe Bryant said, "Talking to Kobe isn't like talking to a seventeen-year-old. It's like talking to a twenty-three-year-old."

Kobe tried to deflect speculation over his future by talking about the present. All he wanted to do was lead Lower Merion to a state title.

He knew that wasn't going to be easy. Coach Downer had decided to challenge his team and had upgraded Lower Merion's schedule. They were due to play some of the best high school teams in the country, including the tough competition at the Beach Ball Classic, a national tournament in South Carolina. In addition, several key players had graduated and Kobe's surrounding cast would be relatively inexperienced. That would allow the opposition to double- and triple-team him every time Lower Merion had the ball.

The Aces stumbled out of the blocks. In an early season meeting against Philadelphia powerhouse Roman Catholic High, Kobe was matched up against Donnie Carr, a player some observers considered his equal. Carr lived in the inner city and was considered to be tougher and more aggressive than Kobe, who some complained played a softer, more "suburban" game. The two had faced each other before in summer camps. Of Kobe, Carr said disdainfully, "If he's a pro, I'm a pro."

A crowd of more than 1,500 turned out to watch the contest. They got their money's worth.

In Lower Merion's defensive scheme, Kobe had to guard Carr one-on-one. But Roman Catholic used a zone against Lower Merion, so when Carr guarded Bryant, he usually had help.

It was a close game. But Roman Catholic did a better job distributing the ball than Lower Merion. Although Bryant played well, he tired in the fourth quarter. After scoring 28 points in the first three periods, in the fourth he missed five of six shots to finish with 30 points. Meanwhile, Carr exploded for 34 and Roman Catholic won, 67–61.

A few weeks later Lower Merion faced the St.

Anthony's Friars of New Jersey, a nationally ranked power. With a big game, Kobe could score his 2,000[th] point in high school, a landmark reached by few other players.

St. Anthony's exposed Lower Merion's lack of depth. Despite missing two starters who had been suspended for disciplinary reasons, the Friars defense collapsed on Kobe, and the other Aces were unable to make up the difference. After Lower Merion hung close for the first three periods, the Friars pulled away in the final quarter to win going away, 62–47. Kobe scored 28 points to go over 2,000 for his career, but he found it an empty achievement. "If we won, getting two thousand would feel awfully good," he said after the game. "Now it just feels like an ordinary accomplishment."

And the Aces were playing like an ordinary team. Downer admitted they were in trouble. Unless the ball was in Kobe's hands, Lower Merion couldn't hang on to it, or score. "There are concerns," he said. "No question about it."

The Aces' dependence on Kobe was made even more apparent in the opening game of the Beach Ball Classic against Ohio's Central Catholic.

Kobe played the best game of his young career, beating Central Catholic almost by himself, as he scored 43 points on 18 of 27 shooting, including three of five from behind the three-point line, and collected 16 rebounds. On defense, he guarded six-foot-eleven standout Jason Collier and held him to only 22 points. But Kobe's teammates scored only 22 points in the 65–60 victory. Downer knew such an imbalance couldn't continue.

In their next game, against Jenks of Oklahoma, the Aces were dumped in overtime, dropping their record to 4–3. Once again, Kobe had been almost the entire show as his teammates stood around and watched him perform. After the game, Downer lit into his team.

He gave a fiery speech that he called "The Cancer of Me." He lambasted his players for not playing team basketball.

"Everything had been me, me, me," he said later. "It had to be about we, we, we."

Downer explained precisely what he expected each player to do. "We did strict role definition," he said. "I told them, 'You can shoot from here, you can shoot from there. This is what we expect of you.' I told them if they couldn't accept their roles, they could turn in their uniforms."

The only player doing what he should was Kobe, which was everything every other player wasn't. As he described it later, "My job was just to plug holes. Whatever the team needed — rebounding, scoring, passing."

Sharpshooter Dan Panagrazio became the team's designated long-range shooter, and gritty Jermaine Griffin their main rebounder. Brendan Pettit was supposed to focus on defense. Point guard Emory Dabney was responsible for getting the ball to his teammates in the right position. The Aces got the message.

They began playing as a team again, which took the pressure off Kobe and, at the same time, made him an even more potent threat as defenses had to focus at least some of their effort on other players. Panagrazio lit it up from outside and Griffin swept the glass. The Aces started blowing their opponents out.

Kobe exploded for 50 points in one 95–64 rout. After another blowout, this one an 84–56 shellacking of Germantown Academy in which Kobe scored 29 and added 17 rebounds, six assists, and five steals, the opposing coach lamented, "They were more than just Kobe." After the win, which made the Aces the first undefeated champions of the Central League, Dan Panagrazio said, "It's amazing. Kobe is not only a great individual, but he makes everyone on the court so much better. He takes us from being a good team to a great team on any night. If we keep this up into the playoffs, there's no limit."

In Kobe's final home game a week later, he took his last bow before the home crowd in spectacular fashion. After Academy Park jumped ahead, 6–4, Kobe took over, scoring the next 12 points in every way possible — three-pointers, dunks, put-backs, and drives. Lower Merion led, 16–6, and never looked back.

Kobe finished with 50 points, matching his career high. So far, he had done everything possible in his high school career except the one thing he wanted most of all — winning a state championship.

Well, winning the state championship and then going straight into the NBA. In the next few weeks, both would be decided.

Chapter Six:
1996

State Champs

During one practice just before the beginning of the state tournament, Coach Downer watched in wonder as Kobe took off from the foul line and jammed in a monstrous dunk. "There are no limits," he said wistfully.

Downer's summation appeared correct as the Aces knifed through the competition to reach the state semifinals with ease. But in order to reach the championship game, they would have to defeat their old nemesis Chester, regarded as perhaps the best defensive team in the state.

The previous season, Chester had embarrassed Kobe and Lower Merion, beating them by 27 points. To remind themselves of that, each member of the Aces wrote the number 27 on his basketball jersey.

Early in the game it appeared as if Chester still had Kobe's number. They swarmed over him, daring him to shoot through double- and triple-teams. Kobe began pressing, and instead of involving his teammates in the game, he tried to do everything himself. Rather than passing the ball to another player, he'd drive and try to cut between defenders and throw up spectacular-looking but incredibly difficult shots. As Kobe said later of his first-half effort, "I was making too many moves. There was too much jelly on my jam."

That style caused his teammates to become spectators. Instead of moving without the ball and trying to get themselves open, they stood around on offense and watched Kobe.

At the end of the first quarter Chester held a narrow lead. At halftime they still led, 31–29. Kobe had shot an uncharacteristic 4-for-14 from the field.

Fortunately, Kobe and his teammates had played much better on the defensive end of the floor. Although Chester had tossed up 43 shots in the first two quarters, few went unchallenged and they managed to make only 14. So far, defense had kept Lower Merion in the game, but everyone watching knew that if Kobe didn't get going in the second half, his dream of winning a state championship would go unfulfilled.

At the half Coach Downer tried to remind his players of their roles and the need to remain patient on offense. He didn't want Kobe to stop shooting, but he wanted to make sure he took his shots in the context of his team's offense.

In the third quarter, Kobe started heating up. Instead of forcing the issue, he took what the defense gave him and started pouring in shots from the outside. On defense, Lower Merion continued to contest every shot, and in the fourth quarter they pulled ahead.

Chester was becoming desperate. Nearly every time Kobe touched the ball, they fouled him. He calmly sank free throw after free throw, helping the Aces to a five-point lead with only two minutes left to play.

But Chester clawed back, tying the game at 61 with only 41 seconds remaining. Then Dan Panagrazio, Lower Merion's second-highest scorer and three-point specialist, went down with a leg injury and was forced from the game.

For the next 41 seconds, the teams went at each other hard. But as they flew up and down the court, fighting for every rebound, neither team could put the ball in the basket. The game entered overtime.

Kobe took over. The exhausted Chester defense couldn't keep up with him anymore. With less than 20 seconds left to play and the Aces leading, 75–69, the ball ended up in Kobe's hands.

He dribbled down the court and the defeated Chester team let him go. At the free throw line he left the court and launched himself into the air. Raising the ball high above his head with one hand, he took aim at the basket.

Slam! He jammed the ball home, providing an exclamation point to the Aces' well deserved, hard fought 77–69 victory. They were going to the finals!

"We knew it was going to be a war coming in," said Kobe later. He had proven to be the best soldier on the court when it had mattered most, scoring 20 of his game-high 39 points in the fourth quarter and overtime to secure the win.

In the finals, Lower Merion faced Erie Cathedral Prep. Erie was determined not to let Kobe run wild in the final.

Erie decided to approach the game with a two-pronged strategy. On offense, they planned to slow everything down and control the tempo. That way they hoped to keep Lower Merion from running and keep the ball out of Kobe's hands on the fast break, where he was most dangerous. And when Lower Merion did get the ball, they decided to double- and triple-team Kobe, knowing that with Panagrazio still sidelined, the Aces didn't really have another scoring threat. The strategy wasn't pretty to watch, but Erie was willing to do anything to win.

The first quarter went just the way Erie had planned. Kobe went scoreless and Erie took a small lead in the low-scoring game.

Coach Downer cautioned his team to remain patient and not try to force things. They listened well, and in the second quarter Kobe managed to shake free for eight points. But the Aces shot only 6-for-22 in the first half and Erie led at halftime, 21–15.

Downer wasn't too concerned. The Aces had been taking good shots; they just hadn't fallen.

He made adjustments. "We tried to give them some different looks," Downer said after the game.

"We tried to get Kobe inside and move him around. The key was to get him in transition."

Erie was taken aback by the change in strategy at the beginning of the second half. Lower Merion scored 11 straight points, only two by Kobe, as his teammates finally found their range. When the horn blew to announce the beginning of the final quarter of Kobe's high school career, Lower Merion led, 37–31.

But Erie regrouped and remained committed to their game plan. They hit a series of long jumpers and led, 41–39, with just over three minutes remaining.

Then Kobe tied the game with two free throws. He added another basket, and with just over a minute remaining, Lower Merion led, 45–43.

Now the pace of the game suddenly turned frantic as each team scrambled to score. Erie missed a jump shot and the Aces rebounded, but quickly turned the ball over.

Erie probed the Lower Merion defense, looking to tie the game. With 30 seconds left one of their players tossed up a runner from the lane. The shot ricocheted off the rim and Kobe soared high above everyone to pull down the rebound. Just as Downer hoped, now Kobe had the ball in transition.

Kobe dribbled quickly upcourt as Erie struggled to stop him. At the top of the key, they swarmed around him. Bryant gave a little fake then flashed a pass to teammate Omar Hatcher, hitting him in full stride. Hatcher laid the ball in and Lower Merion led by four. One foul shot later, the game ended. The scoreboard told the story: Lower Merion 48, Erie 43.

When the final whistle blew, fans rushed the court and the Aces piled upon one another in a big knot. A few moments later, the players took turns mounting a ladder and snipping down the net.

Although Kobe had scored "only" 17 points, he had still been the best player on the court, a player who had made his entire team better and led them to a championship. "This is the final chapter Kobe wanted to write," said Downer. "He deserves it."

Kobe couldn't stop smiling. "Fifteen years from now we'll get together and talk about how we won the state championship," he joked. "But now, I'm gonna take a shower and party."

All joking aside, Kobe knew that now that he had accomplished his goal of winning the state title, the conversation would soon turn to another topic.

Would Kobe Bryant really decide to go straight from high school to the NBA?

Chapter Seven:
1996

Decisions, Decisions

Kobe had but one short month to make up his mind. If he decided to enter the NBA draft, the league required that he declare his intentions in early May, nearly two months before the draft, which was scheduled to take place on June 26. Similarly, if he wanted to attend college he had to decide as quickly as possible because a number of schools, including LaSalle, were holding scholarships for him. It wouldn't be fair to keep them waiting forever.

In newspapers and magazines all over the country, sportswriters and various other basketball personalities debated his options. Most felt that it would be a mistake for Kobe to go straight to the NBA.

Their arguments made a great deal of sense. If he went to the NBA, most people believed he was taking a gamble. If he failed in the NBA or became

Kobe Bryant, star of Lower Merion High School, slams the ball home during a practice session.

Cool and confident, Kobe Bryant announces his plans to enter the NBA draft instead of college.

AP/Wide World Photos

The rookie Laker goes in for a layup against the Jazz during a 1997 playoff game.

A face-splitting grin after a successful — and crowd-pleasing — slam dunk!

All muscle and determination, Kobe Bryant drives the lane against the Houston Rockets.

Eyes never straying from his target, Kobe Bryant focuses on making his shot.

Kobe Bryant powers to the hoop!

All disagreements behind them, Kobe and Shaq hug after a hard-fought win in the 2000 NBA Finals.

Victory! Kobe celebrates with his teammates after they clinch the NBA title.

The championship trophy at his side, Kobe Bryant whoops to the crowd at a celebration the day after the Lakers win the Finals.

Kobe Bryant's Career Stats

YR	G	FGM/A	3PM/A	FTM/A	REB	AST	STL	BLK	TO	PTS
96-97	71	176/422	51/136	136/166	132	91	49	23	112	539
97-98	79	391/913	75/220	363/457	242	199	74	40	157	1220
98-99	50	362/779	27/101	245/292	264	190	72	50	157	996
99-00	66	554/1183	46/144	331/403	416	323	106	62	182	1485
Total	266	1483/3297	199/601	1075/1318	1054	803	301	175	608	4240
Playoffs	50	287/667	39/124	180/236	185	161	53	52	111	793

Kobe Bryant's Career Highlights

1996:
USA Today's High School Player of the Year

1997:
Youngest player to start an NBA game (1/28/97 against Dallas)
NBA Slam Dunk Champion and Rookie All-Star game MVP

1998:
Youngest player to start an All-Star game

2000:
Member of the NBA championship–winning team

injured they worried that he might never attend college and would thereby compromise his future. They also claimed that attending college and experiencing the collegiate lifestyle were important for his personal development and maturity. They cautioned that if he chose to enter the NBA, he might someday regret it. There would be no turning back.

They also cited the experiences of several other young basketball phenoms who had gone straight into the NBA only to have disappointing careers. Center Darryl Dawkins, for example, had entered the NBA out of high school in 1975, becoming a teammate of Joe Bryant's on the Philadelphia 76ers. A remarkable physical talent, Dawkins had lingered on the bench for several seasons before becoming a starting player. And although he had a productive career, he never quite seemed to reach his potential. Many people thought that if Dawkins had attended college for four years he could have developed into an all-time great.

Some observers also expressed concerns about how Kobe's decision might affect other young players. While Kobe was immensely talented, other players without his myriad skills and maturity might incorrectly assume that they, too, could go straight from high school to the NBA. If they miscalculated and the NBA disagreed with their assessment of their skills, their opportunity to attend college to play basketball would be gone, for once a player declares for the draft and signs with an agent, he becomes ineligible for collegiate play. That had, in fact, already happened to several misguided players. Thinking they could go straight to the NBA, several such players didn't take the academic side of high school very seriously. But they were rejected by the NBA and then discovered they were unprepared to move on in a life without basketball.

Others in the basketball community questioned whether Kobe had the talent to make it in the NBA. At six-foot-six and just over 200 pounds, Kobe was what basketball fans sometimes refer to as a "tweener," a player without a true position. They believed that he was too small to play forward in the NBA and didn't yet have the ballhandling or shooting touch to play guard. Jon Jennings, then the director of player development for the Boston Celtics, was one of many NBA insiders who were outspoken in their belief that Kobe wasn't yet an NBA prospect. "It's a total mistake," he told a reporter.

But others believed Kobe could and should go straight to the NBA. They recognized that his background was much different from that of most high school players. They realized that he was more mature and had been exposed to pro basketball his entire life. In Bryant's defense, they cited a number of high school stars who had rejected a chance to go directly into the NBA and chose to attend college, only to be injured or have disappointing careers that harmed their professional prospects. They argued that if the NBA was interested in Kobe, he should jump at the chance and take the money he was certain to be offered. He might not get a second opportunity.

Kobe's parents spent hours discussing his decision with him. But they didn't try to sway him one way or the other. Joe Bryant best summed up their attitude toward their son by saying simply, "Kobe has choices."

Instead of pressuring him, they just tried to make sure that he was aware of the opportunities and risks that each choice entailed. Unlike many other players in his position, for Kobe the money he would earn in the NBA wasn't really an issue. The Bryants were well off and Kobe was under no pressure to join the NBA for monetary reasons.

Meanwhile, as Kobe struggled with his decision, he won a host of honors and awards. His per-game averages of 31 points, 12 rebounds, seven assists, four blocks, and four steals during his senior year made him a consensus all-state selection in Pennsylvania, and he was named to the prestigious *Parade* and McDonald's High School All-American teams. *USA Today* even named him their High School Player of the Year.

Kobe finally reached his decision and held a press conference in the gym at Lower Merion High School just after the final bell on the afternoon of April 29. His classmates raced from class and crowded into the gym to hear the announcement. They were joined by hundreds of media members, the teaching staff, and Kobe's family.

Kobe approached the podium, his shaved head glistening, wearing his best suit jacket and a pair of trousers he'd bought at the last minute, which needed tailoring. The gym turned still as he stood and surveyed the crowd.

Most seventeen-year-olds would have been nervous, but Kobe was cool and assured. He had daydreamed about this moment for years. Before he spoke, he tilted his head, rolled his eyes, and brought his fingers to his chin as if still pondering his decision. Everyone laughed as Kobe's stunt broke the tension.

Then Kobe spoke, clearly and confidently. "I've decided to skip college and take my talent to the NBA," he said.

The gym erupted with applause. His peers had long known of his desire to go to the NBA and they wholeheartedly supported his decision. But Kobe wasn't finished.

"I know I'll have to work extra hard," he said, "and I know this is a big step, but I can do it. It's the opportunity of a lifetime. It's time to seize it while I'm young. I don't know if I can reach the stars or the moon. If I fall off the cliff, so be it." Then he stepped from the podium and embraced his parents as an informal press conference took place.

Kobe's mother reiterated the family's support of their son. "We were going to support him no matter what he chose to do. Whether it was college or the

NBA, we're always going to support him. That's what we do. It was Kobe's decision."

Then she added, "With Kobe, nothing really concerns me about this decision. Like any parent, I have concerns about drugs, alcohol, and fast women, but kids are encountering that in high school.

"But Kobe is a balanced young man," she went on. "He's always stayed focused on what is really important. I don't worry with Kobe or any of my children, because we have a great family foundation."

Then Joe Bryant spoke, admitting, "Hey, I would have liked Kobe to go to school for four years and go to Harvard. But is that reality? This was Kobe's dream. This is his life, so it was his decision."

All of a sudden, Kobe Bryant was big news. His decision to go straight to the NBA was a national story, and Kobe became instantly familiar to most professional basketball fans.

His next step before the draft was to select an agent to represent him in contract negotiations. A few weeks after his announcement, Kobe and his family traveled to New York for a much larger, glitzier press conference at the headquarters of Adidas America, the sneaker and sportswear company. He announced that he had selected the William Morris Agency to represent him, and their first act was to sign him to a multiyear endorsement contract with Adidas. "I'm very excited for this opportunity," said Kobe. "I'm one hundred and ten percent sure I made the right decision."

Adidas CEO Steve Wynne said, "We view Kobe Bryant as one of a new generation of athletes who we think will transform sports in this country. Kobe is a kid with a vision, a kid with a dream. I think his pursuit of that dream is going to be one of the most heartwarming stories in American sports over the next couple of years."

Kobe Bryant had yet to play a minute in the NBA. He didn't even know which team was going to draft him. Yet the deal was reportedly worth nearly ten million dollars. Kobe Bryant was already a millionaire before he had played a second of pro basketball.

A number of NBA teams had scouted Kobe throughout his senior year at Lower Merion, and they now redoubled their efforts. Several teams asked him to attend private workouts so they could assess his skills in a controlled setting. Playing against high school kids was one thing, but performing in a near-empty gym under the scrutiny of NBA coaches and scouts was another.

The Los Angeles Lakers were one of the teams that flew him in for a tryout. While growing up, Kobe had been a huge Lakers fan, primarily because his favorite player, Magic Johnson, had played for them.

But after Johnson announced his retirement in 1991 upon learning he had HIV, the Lakers had rarely exhibited the championship form that marked the Magic years, a fast-breaking, thrilling style of play fans called "Showtime."

NBA legend Jerry West was the Lakers' president. In the 1960s he had led the Lakers to the NBA Finals six times, where they lost each time to the Boston Celtics, before finally capturing a title in 1972. As a player, West was one of the best all-around talents in the history of the league. A six-foot-four guard, West possessed a deadly outside shot, and was able to slash to the hoop, hit teammates with pinpoint passes, and collect rebounds like a big man. He was at his absolute best in pressure situations. Opponents never felt that any lead was safe as long as he was on the court, and he developed a well-deserved reputation as a player who would do anything to win. When the NBA created their red, white, and blue logo featuring a silhouetted basketball player in mid-dribble, the figure was modeled after West. The league could not have made a better choice.

But West had never faced a challenge as difficult as rebuilding the Lakers. Try as he might, he had thus far been unable to build a championship team.

Bryant intrigued West. His youth marked him as a player a team could build around, and his myriad skills reminded West of himself. Moreover, he had heard that Bryant possessed a remarkable work ethic and that the well-mannered young man wasn't likely to be a behavioral risk.

At the same time, West also had his eye on the Orlando Magic's star center, Shaquille O'Neal, who was scheduled to become a free agent. West knew that the great Laker teams of the past had featured not only a great guard, like himself or Magic Johnson, but also a great center, like Wilt Chamberlain or Kareem Abdul-Jabbar. Perhaps, thought West, Bryant and O'Neal might one day form a similar combination that could lead the Lakers to a championship. If everything worked out, he hoped to acquire both players.

But West still wanted to see Bryant for himself. At the workout he stood on the sidelines as Bryant performed for Laker coaches, displaying all of his skills. Near the end of the workout, they asked Bryant to play one-on-one against Laker assistant coach and one-time NBA defensive specialist Michael Cooper.

Bryant played well against Cooper, and his performance gave West a glimpse of what he believed was the most important quality for any player to have — his heart. He could see the desire contained in Bryant's game as he relentlessly attacked the basket on offense and challenged Cooper on defense.

West was stunned by what he saw. He had heard that Bryant was good, but the workout really opened his eyes. He later said, "He was the most skilled player we've ever worked out, the kind of skill you don't see very often. He has the potential to be an All-Star."

The workout left him convinced that Bryant could be the player the Lakers needed, particularly if they were able to acquire O'Neal as well. But there was just one problem. It wasn't going to be easy for the Lakers to get either player, much less both of them. West knew he would have to outbid every team in the league for the services of O'Neal. And the Lakers were saddled with a late pick in the first round of the draft. Chances were slim that Bryant would still be available.

Although it was no secret that Bryant hoped to play for the Lakers, his desire would have little influence on who picked him in the NBA draft. His options would be few, for if he didn't sign a contract with the team that picked him, he wouldn't be able to play in the league at all. It was that simple.

On draft day Kobe was nervous. Most observers expected him to be chosen somewhere between the tenth and fifteenth picks in the first round, long before the Lakers got to select. Yet as talented as he was, most teams still considered him a "project," a player who wouldn't be able to contribute for several seasons, and most NBA teams couldn't afford to be that patient with a number-one draft pick. Kobe hoped that would allow him to slip down far enough for the Lakers to take him.

He watched nervously as the first dozen teams

made their picks, selecting college stars like Allen Iverson, who could help out immediately. Then he watched NBA commissioner David Stern approach the podium at NBA draft headquarters and announce, "With the thirteenth pick of the draft the Charlotte Hornets select Kobe Bryant of Lower Merion High School."

The Charlotte Hornets?

Chapter Eight:
1996–1997

Showboat or Showtime?

Coach Dave Cowens of the Charlotte Hornets had once been a star center for the Boston Celtics. Although Cowens had been smaller than most NBA big men, he was aggressive and tenacious. He had made a career by outplaying bigger men.

He had been a particular thorn in the side of the Lakers' Kareem Abdul-Jabbar. Now, by picking Bryant, Cowens had stuck it to the Lakers once again.

Kobe and his family were upset, but realized there was little they could do. It appeared as if Bryant's career would begin in Charlotte, an idea that didn't excite him very much.

That's because Cowens didn't think Bryant was ready for the NBA. After drafting him, he called Bryant "a kid," and openly questioned how much he would play. If Cowens believed that, thought

Bryant, then why had he bothered drafting him in the first place?

The answer to that question soon became clear. Cowens knew that the Lakers wanted Bryant and that Bryant wanted to play for the Lakers. He also knew the Lakers were expected to make an all-out effort to sign Shaquille O'Neal, which would make current Laker center Vlade Divac expendable. He wanted Divac and planned to use Bryant to get the player he really wanted.

It was a savvy move on Cowens's part, but a risky proposition for the Lakers. O'Neal had yet to sign with L.A., and West didn't want to trade Divac until he had acquired O'Neal. But he knew if he didn't go after Bryant right away, the Hornets might well trade him elsewhere.

As a player, West had gambled many times. Now he did so again. When Cowens dangled Bryant in front of the Lakers, West couldn't resist. He traded Divac for rights to the young player.

In mid-July Bryant flew to Los Angeles to sign the standard rookie contract, worth 3.5 million dollars. At the airport, while he waited for his luggage, a stranger approached the tall young man and said,

"You must be a basketball player. Who do you play for?"

Without thinking, Bryant started to answer, "Lower Merion." Then he caught himself. "I guess I'm a Laker," he said with a smile. He liked the way that sounded.

"I'm very excited to be here," said Bryant after the signing ceremony. "It's a dream come true to come to a team like L.A. that has a great history. It was a team I looked up to growing up."

Jerry West was similarly delighted, but he cautioned that Bryant was unlikely to be an overnight sensation. "In five or six years the people of Los Angeles will be talking of him in very high terms. We know there will be some growing pains in the process, but we are prepared to accept this challenge."

Kobe's father, mother, and sister Shaya soon joined him in California. Joe Bryant even gave up his job at LaSalle. They realized that Kobe was only seventeen and would need a lot of support. They all moved into a house in the southern California hills. The house had a spectacular view, with the ocean on one side and the city on another. Kobe's room overlooked the Pacific Ocean. But he tried to stay focused on his goals.

"I won't be doing a lot of hanging out after the games," said Bryant. "I'll be going home to do homework and play video games and chow down on a home cooked meal." Bryant had already made the decision to start taking college courses in business to help him manage his new fortune.

Meanwhile, Jerry West's gamble paid off. He was able to sign Shaquille O'Neal to a contract worth an incredible 123 million dollars. The Lakers had paid a stiff price, but West had acquired the two players he believed could lead the Lakers to a championship.

Bryant was still a kid who just loved to play basketball. Before training camp started, he traveled to Venice Beach, just outside L.A., where some of the best pickup games in the area were played. He wanted to be ready for training camp.

But during one game in early September, he took a tumble and cracked a small bone in his left wrist. Some members of the press questioned his maturity for playing in an unorganized game.

Although the Lakers weren't thrilled with his injury, West understood, saying, "This guy will play in a Little League tournament. It doesn't bother me. He loves to play basketball and is one of the most dedicated players I have ever seen." He appreciated Bryant's unbridled passion for basketball.

Still, when training camp opened in October Bryant was unable to play. All he could do was run and participate in drills that didn't require him to handle the ball.

Kobe took camp seriously and worked hard to fit in. Veteran Lakers were curious about the young player.

He immediately impressed them with his work ethic, but his inability to participate in workouts left him far behind. He couldn't really learn the offense or determine where he fit in on the Laker team.

With O'Neal playing center, everything was changing and the team had to learn to play a whole new way. The veteran players were more concerned with learning their roles than they were with how Bryant was adjusting.

He also didn't quite know how to behave around the veteran club. After practice, many Lakers took full advantage of their celebrity status in the city, going to clubs and hanging out together. Kobe was too young to get into most of the nightclubs and didn't care to spend his time in them, anyway. He kept to himself, stayed quiet, and tried to learn by watching.

Some members of the team thought he was aloof and didn't quite know what to make of him. Bryant knew that until he had a chance to play and demonstrate his skills, it would be hard to fit in. Besides, although he wasn't intimidated being around the other players, he was cautious about succumbing to the NBA lifestyle. His priorities began and ended with basketball.

But that didn't make him immune to the usual hazing and pranks veterans pull on rookies. At a team dinner they made Bryant sing and teased him about his friendship with the pop singer and TV actress Brandy, whom he had taken to his senior prom. They weren't trying to be mean, but Bryant was sensitive to the teasing.

Near the end of training camp his wrist finally healed and he began to get some playing time. He demonstrated confidence in his game, but also showed that he still had a lot to learn.

Bryant played the same way he had in high school. He thought nothing of going one-on-one against players of greater size and more experience, or taking the important shot. His teammates immediately nicknamed him "Showboat."

The name stung. Bryant considered himself a team player. But he was so confident that when he saw an opening, he tried to exploit it. He just wasn't accustomed to playing in a system where every other player was a legitimate option.

He had particular trouble on defense. He often went for the steal or went after rebounds he had no chance of getting. As a result, he sometimes left his own man wide open.

That wasn't the way Laker coach Del Harris wanted things done. He wanted Bryant to stay within the offense, work the ball inside to O'Neal, and play team defense. Although he knew Bryant would be a great player someday, Harris also knew that his job depended upon his ability to win now. He couldn't afford to wait for Bryant and really wasn't concerned with getting him playing time. He was far more occupied with the task of getting his starters to learn to play with a force like O'Neal. The club had undergone a complete changeover since the previous year and only five players remained from the 1995–96 team.

When the season started, Bryant only played during garbage time, when the Lakers were far ahead or far behind. Even then, the instant he made a mistake, Harris pulled him from the game. Kobe didn't get his first basket until the fifth game of the season.

With O'Neal at center, everyone expected the Lakers to win immediately, and in fact they did get off to a hot start. That made it even more difficult for Bryant to get meaningful minutes. Harris was far more concerned with giving his key players more time playing with one another than he was with working Bryant into the lineup.

Bryant tried to be philosophical about it, telling the press, "My father keeps telling me my time will come." But for a basketball junkie like Bryant, sitting on the bench was hard to deal with. Some members of the press who had thought it was a mistake for Bryant to skip college took note of his lack of playing time and began whispering, "I told you so."

Behind the scenes, Lakers president Jerry West

was putting some pressure on Harris to play Bryant more often, but the coach was resistant. The Lakers were on pace to win more than 50 games, and he didn't want to risk disrupting his team just to give Bryant some experience.

When the league broke to celebrate the annual All-Star weekend, the Lakers led the Pacific Division. Due more to his name than his numbers, Bryant was selected to participate in the Rookie All-Star game; a showcase for younger players played the day before the All-Star game.

Bryant was pumped up about finally playing. The game would be broadcast nationally, giving many NBA fans their first real look at Bryant.

In the free-form, 30 minute contest, which more resembled a pickup game than a regular-season NBA contest, Bryant flourished, outscoring more heralded rookies like Allen Iverson to lead all scorers with 31 points.

But he saved the best for the slam-dunk contest. Although the contest had once attracted the game's biggest stars, they had begun to shy away. As a result, young players like Bryant were invited to participate.

He started slowly and barely made it to the final

round of four players. Then Bryant rose to the occasion. As he had done so many times in his high school career, he saved the best for last.

Starting on the left side, he charged the basket, went into the air, and seemed to hang in defiance of gravity. As he did, he passed the ball from one hand to the other *between his legs,* then spun to the basket and slammed the ball home! It was a spectacular move.

The crowd jumped to its feet, as did judge Julius Erving, who as a player had been best known for his artistic dunking style. Jazzed up by the crowd, Bryant bounced to midcourt, stood before the judges, and flexed his slender body like a bodybuilder.

The crowd roared again. To no one's surprise, Bryant won the contest.

But none of his All-Star weekend success mattered when the regular season resumed. Bryant continued to play only five or ten minutes a game even as O'Neal was lost for over a month to injury.

But another injury finally gave him a chance to play. Point guard Nick Van Exel went down and shooting guard Derek Fisher took over the point. Harris had little choice but to pair Bryant in the backcourt with Fisher.

For the first time all year, Laker fans got a glimpse of the future. The team won five of the six games he started. Bryant proved that he could score — and the opposition discovered that at times they had to double-team him. Even better, he demonstrated that he was learning what to do in such situations, as he rarely forced a shot and proved adept at finding the open man.

Although he went back to the bench when Van Exel returned, Bryant's playing time increased as Harris began to realize he could provide some instant offense. He ended up averaging 15 minutes per game over the course of the season. O'Neal returned to the lineup and the Lakers made the playoffs easily, finishing 56–26, just a game behind Seattle SuperSonics for second place in the Pacific Division.

In the first round, the Lakers blew out the Portland Trailblazers, winning the best-of-five playoff three games to one. Bryant hardly played in the three Laker wins, but in game three, with the Lakers trailing, he had come off the bench to keep things close by scoring 22.

In the next round, against the Utah Jazz, the Lakers lost the first two games of the best-of-five series and again Bryant played only a few minutes. But opportunity came in game three once again.

The Lakers jumped ahead early, but turned cold as Utah began to make a move in the fourth quarter. Harris recalled Bryant's performance against Portland and he put him in the lineup, looking for some points.

Bryant proved he was becoming an explosive scorer. He scored 17 points in the final period as he kept the pressure on Utah by driving to the basket again and again. They responded with fouls, and he coolly sank 13 of 14 free throws to secure the 104–84 win.

If L.A. didn't win game four, their season was over. Harris decided to go with the hot hand and Bryant played much of the game.

With the Lakers nursing an 87–85 lead with less than a minute remaining, Jazz veteran guard John Stockton went one-on-one against Bryant. When the rookie went for a fake, Stockton blew past him to score a layup and tie the game with 11 seconds remaining.

L.A. called time-out. O'Neal had fouled out and the Lakers needed someone to take the final shot. Harris decided that someone would be Bryant. He told his team to get him the ball and get out of the way. The decision showed a lot of confidence in the rookie.

L.A. inbounded the ball to Kobe and his teammates scattered, leaving him isolated on one side of the court. He moved toward the basket, pulled up, and from fourteen feet shot a potentially game-winning jumper. He had made the same shot thousands of times while playing shadow ball.

But this time, there was a national television audience, thousands of fans in the stands, and a hand in his face. The ball fell short. Air ball! The game entered overtime.

Bryant was uncharacteristically unnerved. In the extra period he shot three more times, and three more times he missed the basket entirely. The Jazz won going away, and the partisan Utah crowd hooted Bryant and his teammates off the court.

The press questioned Harris's decision to put the ball in Bryant's hands in crunch time, and the coach snapped, "All year I get criticized for not playing him and now I'm criticized for playing him."

But no one felt worse than Kobe Bryant did. After returning to Los Angeles, the next morning Bryant went to the gym and began working on his second season in the NBA. His rookie year was over.

Chapter Nine:

1997-98

One Step at a Time

Bryant knew he had to work harder if he was ever to achieve the level of success he expected from himself in the NBA. In addition to his time spent in the gym, he added a grueling weight-training regimen to his fitness routine so he could become bigger and stronger. He also played for the team the Lakers sponsored in the L.A. Summer Pro League, coached by former player Larry Drew.

Although Bryant's performance in the playoffs seemed to indicate that he would play a key role on the team in the upcoming season, as he played in the summer league it became apparent that wasn't necessarily the case. The Lakers tried to put restrictions on his game. They didn't want him to score as much as they wanted him to pass.

Bryant tried to adjust, but he found the transition

difficult. He was convinced that his talents were best used as a scorer, but the Laker offense was increasingly focused on getting the ball to O'Neal inside. It was a slowdown style that Bryant felt uncomfortable with.

He tried his best to fit in. But in the preseason it became clear that Coach Harris planned to use Bryant off the bench as a sixth man, either a shooting guard or small forward.

While Bryant was disappointed that he wasn't in the starting lineup, the role suited him. Since he was no longer playing the point, he wasn't expected to distribute the ball. And he often entered the game while either O'Neal or the Lakers other main scoring option, Eddie Jones, was taking a breather. Bryant's job was to energize the team and put the ball in the basket.

That was something he was beginning to do in ever more spectacular fashion. He'd grown an inch and become stronger in the off-season, and his offensive skills began drawing comparisons to Michael Jordan. He looked even taller, as he let his hair grow out into a distinctive, short Afro.

In one amazing sequence, Bryant showed that he

had skills that perhaps even Jordan didn't have. In a preseason game against Washington, Bryant got the ball in transition and charged down the court, freeing himself from his defender with a nifty crossover dribble.

He had two options. He could either shoot the short twelve- to fourteen-foot jump shot or drive to the basket, where Washington's six-foot-nine forward Ben Wallace stood blocking his way.

The situation was not unlike that which he had faced at the end of the game against Utah. All summer long he had replayed the sequence in his head, trying to figure out why he had missed the shot. He finally came to the conclusion that he had shot an air ball because he had really wanted to drive straight to the basket. He hadn't because he had worried about committing a foul or being accused of being too flashy. In short, he had talked himself out of doing what came naturally, out of being Kobe Bryant. That lack of confidence had probably led to the three air balls he had shot in overtime, as well.

He was determined not to let that happen again. Without hesitation he went right at Wallace.

The big man was in perfect position — in a slight

crouch in case he had to jump up to block a shot, with his arms and legs spread wide to keep Bryant from cutting past him. There was no apparent opening to the basket for Kobe Bryant.

But that didn't stop him. He took the ball in his hand, took a quick, hard step, and went up . . .

. . . and up, and up, and up. Legs spread wide, Bryant went straight at, then over the befuddled defender, who ducked slightly as Bryant soared over his head and jammed the ball through the hoop!

His teammates, the opposition, and the fans sat stunned in their seats for a moment. Then, as the crowd roared, Bryant's teammates looked incredulously at one another. The sheepish Wallace spun and looked around as if wondering where Bryant had gone. But he was already back down to earth, racing down the court. It was a move that no one, not even Michael Jordan, could have made.

When the regular season started, the Lakers opened with a rush, winning their first eleven games. O'Neal dominated the inside and Bryant came off the bench to score almost at will, averaging nearly 20 points a game, a remarkable total for a player who was usually on the court for only half the game. While some observers groused that he was still out of control and still failed to play within the team concept, the results were undeniable. The Lakers were winning.

The comparisons to Jordan continued when the Lakers and Bulls met for the first time that season in a game the press hyped as a meeting of the past and future of the NBA. Although Chicago won by 20 and Jordan poured in 36 points, Bryant held his own against the legendary star, hitting for a career-high 33 points and making Jordan work for every shot.

Basketball fans throughout the country were beginning to realize what Bryant's teammates already knew; he was becoming the most exciting player in the NBA. "He amazes me," said teammate Nick Van Exel. "I see him every day and he still amazes me."

Added Eddie Jones, "Every play, you look at him and you wonder, 'What's next?' I would pay money just to watch Kobe play for ten seconds."

The fans confirmed Jones's estimation of Bryant when they voted for the NBA All-Star team. Kobe Bryant, the sixth man on his own team, collected more votes than any other player, out-polling even Michael Jordan to earn a starting berth on the

Western Conference squad. It was an unprece-dented achievement for a nineteen-year-old player.

Although a few members of the press sniped that Bryant didn't deserve the honor, the other All-Stars were well aware that his popularity was good for the league and they welcomed him.

The game was held in New York's Madison Square Garden, smack in the middle of the world's media capital, guaranteeing that every move Bryant made would be scrutinized. Not many nineteen-year-olds could handle that much pressure, but Bryant tried to remain cool, although even he had to admit at a press conference before the game, "My body's numb, my heart's racing."

Observers were again touting the game as a matchup between Jordan and Bryant. The two play-ers realized that's what the fans wanted to see and tried to play up to the hype.

It helped that in All-Star games teams play lit-tle defense. In such a setting, Bryant's and Jordan's skills were on full display. The two players raced up and down the court, matching each other with shot after spectacular shot.

One shot Bryant made in the third quarter still

has fans talking. The West had the ball on a fast break, and Kobe led the charge down the court.

He could have passed to a teammate, and perhaps he should have, but instead he chose to give the crowd their money's worth. He decided to take the shot himself.

In full stride he first hid the ball behind his back with his left hand as he looked the opposite way, then took it out and jumped, out of control and tumbling, before tossing up a crazy, no-look hook shot over his head, an impossible shot that somehow went in.

But that was the end of the show. Western Conference coach George Karl pulled Bryant from the game in the fourth quarter in favor of some veteran players. Bryant ended up with 18 points and 6 rebounds in 22 minutes of play against the NBA's best. But Jordan, who played most of the game and scored 23 points, earned MVP honors for the victorious East.

Bryant didn't mind. "I just wanted to sit back, observe the whole thing," he said, adding, "This is the most fun I've ever had. I'm kind of sad it's over."

Those words would prove to be prophetic, for the

first weeks of the second half of the season weren't much fun for either Kobe Bryant or the Lakers. Illness and injury sent the Lakers into a slide, and after his All-Star performance, Bryant suddenly found himself the object of increased attention by opposing defenses. His shooting suffered, and he seemed to be forcing his game and appeared out of sync. Coach Harris began turning to other options on his bench and Bryant's playing time dropped. Instead of being called on to provide instant offense, he was being used primarily for his defense.

The team managed to right itself in the final six weeks of the season, winning twenty-two of their final twenty-five to finish with a record of 61–21, just a game behind the Utah Jazz and Chicago Bulls for the best record in the league. But while the Lakers thrived, Bryant withdrew, and the player who appeared on the verge of becoming the best in the game at midseason was on the verge of disappearing.

People began to openly wonder whether the Lakers were actually a better team without Bryant. In the first round of the playoffs, against Portland, he played sporadically, getting a handful of minutes in one game, then playing nearly all of the next. The

Lakers won easily to advance to the next round, versus Seattle.

Bryant played even less against Seattle, getting little more than garbage time as the Lakers again swept to victory. It appeared as if the team might have an appointment with the Bulls in the Finals.

But the Utah Jazz got in the way. They exposed the Lakers on defense, as their highly disciplined offense, keyed by Karl Malone and John Stockton, ran the Lakers ragged. And on defense the Jazz, unlike most other teams, didn't just focus on O'Neal. They pressured everyone, and the Lakers simply couldn't score. In limited time, Bryant was no more successful than his teammates.

By the time of their final defeat in the four-game sweep, the Lakers were sniping at one another and at Coach Harris. Bryant had withdrawn during the second half of the season and hardly knew what to think anymore. As he later admitted, "I've been humbled."

His future would depend upon how he reacted to that experience.

Chapter Ten:
1998–1999

The Lost Season

When a reporter asked Bryant how he planned to spend his off-season, he responded simply, "Basketball. That's all."

Unfortunately, much of his work was done in vain. The 1998–99 NBA season was a disaster from the very beginning. The players union's contract with the owners had expired and the owners enforced a "lockout," effectively putting the season on hold. The two sides fought each other for months as the season slipped away.

When the lockout finally ended in January of 1999, the Lakers were in disarray. After a falling out with Laker management, guard Nick Van Exel had been traded and most Laker players — though not Bryant — returned to play out of shape and unprepared. The result was turmoil from the very beginning.

During a hurried preseason practice and exhibition slate, the Lakers struggled to prepare for the upcoming season. What discipline the team had displayed the previous season quickly eroded.

Practices were a disaster. Bryant was accustomed to playing hard and went all out, an approach that angered many of his teammates, who felt he was trying to show them up. During one two-on-two session with O'Neal, Corie Blount, and Derek Fisher, O'Neal and Bryant had a confrontation that resulted in a brief scuffle. Although the altercation took place because each player was tired at the end of the long scrimmage, it revealed a problem between the two. While neither player cared to talk about it, observers hinted that O'Neal was jealous of Bryant's tendency to take over on offense, which he felt left him out far too often and cost him shots. Bryant, on the other hand, thought that O'Neal's work ethic didn't match his incredible physical skills. In short, neither player really respected the other.

O'Neal and Bryant stopped talking and people

wondered if it would ever be possible for the two stars to learn to play with one another. If they didn't, they would never win a championship together.

The ill feeling between the two spilled over into the regular season, as did the Lakers' disorganized play. In reality, both players were at fault, for each had always been the focus of every team he had played on. Added to that was the fact that at age nineteen, Bryant didn't have much in common with his teammates, who went out together after the game and forged friendships off the court. Bryant's best friends were still members of his own family and old friends from high school.

The club got off to a rocky start, and after only eleven games Del Harris was fired and replaced by former Laker player Kurt Rambis. At the same time the club signed controversial forward and master rebounder Dennis Rodman. Although Rodman was incredibly valuable on the court, his flamboyant lifestyle had often been a distraction.

But the changes made little difference, and after another twelve games the Lakers decided to retool, trading Eddie Jones and Elden Campbell to Charlotte for long-range shooter Glen Rice and forward

J. R. Reid. Then Rodman, in a dizzying week of controversy, retired, unretired, and was released. Some pundits suggested the team install a revolving door leading to the locker room.

The team split into several cliques, each of which blamed the others for the club's erratic performance. O'Neal still wanted the offense to revolve around him, and Rice had a hard time adjusting to a system where he was usually the second or third option. In Charlotte, he had been his team's go-to guy, the player who got the ball at crunch time. In Los Angeles, that player was O'Neal.

Bryant felt frustrated. He thought the Laker offense held him back and kept him from playing his game and using all his skills.

On the court, the team's internal troubles became obvious. Everyone was still trying to learn what was expected of him, but they weren't really playing together. When the Lakers struggled or the offense broke down, Bryant looked to score, which only increased the feeling of friction of the team. Too often, Bryant had the ball twenty or twenty-five feet from the basket, juking and faking and dribbling while his teammates just stood around unsure of what he was going to do next. And when Coach Rambis tried to initiate some changes in the club's offense to accommodate both O'Neal and Bryant, the team often ignored him.

But even as the club continued to struggle, Bryant's playing time increased. He moved into the starting lineup, splitting time between the guard and forward positions. As he got the opportunity to play, he cut loose and wowed fans at L.A.'s Great Western Forum with his stunning athleticism and leaping ability. Bryant often played to the crowd, trying to top each spectacular shot with an even better one.

It was entertaining, but did nothing to help team chemistry. O'Neal and other veteran players felt left out, and Bryant was estranged from his teammates. The local media went wild reporting on the Lakers' ongoing soap opera, as O'Neal intimated that he thought Bryant alone was the cause of the team's problems. After each game or practice, Bryant went one way and the rest of the team went another. In an understatement, Joe Bryant said, "It's been a difficult year for my son."

Yet somehow, despite everything, the Lakers had

enough talent to win more than they lost. But critics noted that the Lakers didn't appear to have a coherent plan on offense. When their jump shots fell, which opened up the inside for O'Neal, they won. But when they didn't, the opposition could double-team O'Neal and pick off rebounds, often holding the Lakers to just a single shot. When that happened, the Lakers had a hard time scoring and usually lost.

Bryant finished the regular season with a scoring average of nearly 20 points per game. Los Angeles faced the Houston Rockets, a team in even more disarray than the Lakers, in the first round of the playoffs.

In the first two games of the series, the Lakers looked like a team that had finally learned to play together. Bryant shut down Rocket star Scottie Pippen, and the Lakers swept the first two games.

But when Bryant got in foul trouble in game three, Pippen went wild, scoring 37 points as the Rockets won. Then the Lakers pulled a surprise in game four.

Bryant and O'Neal spent much of the first half

passing to each other for easy baskets, and the Lakers jumped out way ahead and won with ease, eliminating the Rockets. It was the way it was supposed to be, and gave everyone a glimpse of just how good the Lakers could be if O'Neal and Bryant learned to play together, just as Jerry West had once learned to play with Wilt Chamberlain, and Magic Johnson with Kareem Abdul-Jabbar.

"All those stories about me and Shaq, you can throw in the garbage," said Bryant afterward. "Look at us. We play great together."

The victory sent the Lakers up against the San Antonio Spurs in the next round. With their twin towers of Tim Duncan and David Robinson, the Spurs had the manpower to match up against O'Neal under the basket. When they did, the Lakers appeared confused. Rice and Bryant both reacted by trying to go one-on-one in an attempt to generate some offense. But the Spurs continued to dominate play underneath the basket and control the tempo of the game.

With O'Neal in constant foul trouble and the rest of the team shooting poorly, the Lakers battled hard but couldn't manage to overcome the Spurs. And for the second straight year Kobe Bryant missed several important shots late in close games, including two bricks from the free throw line that cost his team a chance to win game three. The Spurs defeated the Lakers in four straight games. The season was over.

Finally.

Chapter Eleven:
1999–2000

Triangle Turnaround

It was obvious to everyone that the Lakers needed to change something if they were ever going to reach their potential. Some observers speculated that either O'Neal or Bryant would be traded. Or perhaps both players would be shipped off and the Lakers would embark on a total rebuilding program.

But Jerry West still believed the Lakers had all the players in place to win a championship. What they needed was someone to get it all to work together.

As coach of the Chicago Bulls, Phil Jackson had developed a reputation as a man who could get talented players with big egos to play together. For the Bulls, despite the presence of Michael Jordan, hadn't managed to win a championship until Jackson became coach.

He had installed an offense known as the triangle, a strategy that took advantage of both Jordan's skills and those of star forward Scottie Pippen. As a result, he had gotten the most from each player.

The triangle, which had been developed in collegiate basketball, was new to pro basketball. Traditionally, most pro offenses had been designed to isolate a particular player one-on-one. As a team moved the ball across half-court, players set up in specific positions on the court and the point guard, out on top, called out the play and put it in motion, usually by a pass to another player. But if the defense broke up the play or it was disrupted for another reason, the player with the ball usually had few options. The ball was sent back out and another play was called. The role of each player was strictly defined.

But the triangle was different. Simply put, it demanded that the players react to what the defense did, depending on the motion and movement of each player. Each player had to be able to read the defense, learn how to react, and pass to the open man.

Although the offense was demanding, it wasn't

rigid. There was plenty of room for creativity. When it worked, it was beautiful to watch as the ball zipped back and forth and players ran and cut all over the floor until someone worked free and finished the play, usually with a wide open jump shot or a layup or dunk from in close. In the team concept, it allowed the individual player to flourish and stay involved.

Jordan and the Bulls had worked the offense to perfection. But that hadn't been the only key to their success.

Jackson's personality was much different from that of most NBA coaches. He viewed the game of basketball in human terms and appreciated it for its capacity to bring individuals together in pursuit of a common goal, an approach that he saw as symbolic of the way people should live. While many had first scoffed at his approach, his record of success in Chicago was undeniable.

After Michael Jordan had retired, Jackson had re-signed and sat out the 1998–99 season. Now he was ready to return to coaching. He let the Lakers know he wanted to come to Los Angeles. In Bryant and

O'Neal, he saw two players he believed would thrive in the triangle, for each could both pass the ball and score. West agreed. Rambis simply didn't have the respect of his players. After letting him go, West named Jackson coach. West believed that if anyone could get O'Neal and Bryant to work together, it was Jackson.

Critics questioned the hiring, saying that the only reason Jackson had been so successful in Chicago was because Michael Jordan was a member of the Bulls. Getting the Lakers to play together, they argued, would be an entirely different challenge.

But O'Neal and Bryant, for all their differences, were actually quite similar. Each had been expected to be a star since entering the league, and each had been something of a disappointment. Both players were still referred to in terms of their potential, as if neither had yet reached it.

At the same time, they shared a common goal. Each wanted to win very badly. Their reputations had taken a beating and each player knew that the only way to silence his critics would be to win a championship. It helped immeasurably that Jackson already had the respect of both players. After all, his record spoke for itself. And Bryant and O'Neal had been dissatisfied with Harris and Rambis, neither of whom had been able to enforce any team discipline. This had led each player to feel that he needed to take over on the court, a major cause of the friction between the two. Under Jackson, Bryant and O'Neal hoped things would be different.

During training camp each player deferred to Coach Jackson. When the rest of the Lakers saw how intent Bryant and O'Neal were on giving their new coach some respect, they fell in line. They listened patiently as he explained their roles in the triangle, and they accepted criticism each time he stopped play and explained what someone had done wrong. As Jackson explained to his players, "I have to tell you about a mistake so you know you made a mistake. But it's not personal criticism." Everything was done for the good of the team and the betterment of all.

Bryant thrived under Jackson's instruction, saying later that Jackson's approach had allowed him to realize when he was making mistakes without being told. Now, he said, "I know when I mess up and I say, 'OK, hold on, I've got to step back.'"

To everyone's surprise, by the time the regular season opened the Lakers were running the triangle as if they had been doing so for years. O'Neal had never been more dominant under the basket, as the offense prevented defenses from packing in around him. When he got the ball in the low post the defense was usually still in transition, allowing him an open route to the basket that often resulted in monstrous dunks. At times he was simply unstoppable, scoring at will and ripping down rebound after rebound.

At the same time, Bryant had never played with so much control. His speed, quickness, and ballhandling skills were perfectly suited for the constant motion required by the triangle. It freed him on the outside for jump shots, for drives to the basket, and, significantly, to make crowd-pleasing passes not seen on the Lakers since Magic Johnson had been a star. For the first time, Bryant began to be recognized not just for his scoring ability, but for his ability to create shots for other players.

Yet the offense still allowed him an outlet for his creative urges. He'd often find himself wide open with a clear path to the lane, the perfect situation to throw down one of his spectacular jams. Basketball had become fun again.

Before the season was a month old, it was obvious that the Lakers would be the team to beat for the NBA championship. The controversy and frustrations of the previous season melted away. O'Neal and Bryant developed a healthy respect for one another and even became friends. On one occasion, when Bryant got involved in a scuffle with New York Knick Chris Childs and elbowed him in the face, O'Neal was outspoken in his defense, saying, "Everyone knows Kobe's a clean-cut kid. He was protecting himself."

It was "Showtime" in Los Angeles again. The Lakers romped to the Pacific Division title with the league's best record, 67–15. O'Neal was named to the All-NBA first team, and Kobe Bryant made the second team, as well as the All-Defensive first team.

The team's performance earned them home-court advantage throughout the playoffs. They put it to good use as they surged to the Finals, beating the Sacramento Kings, Phoenix Suns, and Portland Trailblazers in succession to earn the right to play the Indiana Pacers for the NBA championship.

The Pacers were tough, experienced, and talented. Under their coach, former NBA great Larry Bird, they had been knocking on the door of the NBA championship for several seasons, only to fall just short. Led by guard Reggie Miller, they were a rugged defensive team known for their clutch shooting and never-say-die attitude. Although the Lakers were favored to win, some thought the Pacers might just pull off an upset. Bird had announced he would retire after the season, and the Pacers wanted to send their coach out a winner.

But the Lakers sent a message in game one. Working the triangle to perfection, they fed the ball to Shaq over and over again and he came up big, scoring 43 points and pulling down 19 rebounds. "When he gets in that kind of groove," said Bryant, "you've got to get the ball to him." The Lakers won, 104–87.

In game two, L.A. got off to another quick start, playing great team basketball. Bryant didn't attempt his first shot, a seventeen-foot jumper, until there were only three minutes left in the first quarter. He went up high as the Pacers' Jalen Rose jumped up to try to block his shot.

Bryant was too quick and got his shot off clean.

But as it soared through the hoop for two points, he came back down to earth and his right foot landed on Rose's foot. Bryant's foot turned grotesquely and he fell hard, a wince on his face. He got back up and tried to shake off the injury, but left the game a few moments later with a badly sprained ankle.

Fortunately, Glen Rice took up the scoring slack and Brian Shaw stepped in for Bryant and led L.A. to a 111–104 victory. But with Bryant's status for game three unclear, Rice spoke for everyone after the game when he said, "When you lose a key player, one of the things you have to do is come together collectively. We may well be short again. Guys have to step up again."

Bryant was crushed by the injury and did everything he could to prepare for game three, but was unable to play. Without him, the Lakers lost, 100–91. Suddenly, the Pacers seemed poised to take control of the series.

Few people expected Bryant to play in game four. He tried the ankle in practice but found it was still too sore. Many observers expected him to miss the remainder of the Finals.

An hour before game four, Bryant was still receiving treatment from team doctors. Although there was little danger he would hurt his foot more by playing on it, he was still in significant pain.

But when Bryant took the court before the game, his adrenaline started pumping and the ankle, heavily taped, began to feel better. He told Jackson he could play, and the coach put him in the starting lineup. The Lakers knew they couldn't let the Pacers tie the series.

The two teams played each other even, neither giving in. When Shaq missed a short jump hook at the buzzer, the game was tied, 104–104; it was going to overtime.

Bryant's ankle hadn't been much of a factor thus far. He'd played well, but during time-outs could be seen noticeably limping. Now he had to play extra time.

Just a few minutes into overtime, the Lakers received a severe blow. Battling for a rebound, O'Neal was called for his sixth foul and had to leave the game.

Lakers fans groaned. O'Neal had been playing a

great game and his loss gave the Pacers a huge advantage.

But as O'Neal trudged to the bench, Kobe Bryant approached him, winked, and whispered something. As Bryant said later, "This is the game you dream about as you're growing up. You lose yourself in the moment. You're consumed by the game."

Coach Jackson sensed the time for L.A. to win was now. He later said, "I broke down our offense and went to an open-floor game for Kobe."

Indiana immediately went on the attack. Their center, Rik Smits, hit a jump hook to draw the Pacers to within one of L.A., 112–111. Then Bryant got the ball.

He never thought about his late misses in the playoffs in the past. He drove down the court, stopped, stutter-stepped, and faked a drive. Then, as the defense reacted, he stepped back to give himself some room and calmly took a jump shot.

Swish! Nothing but net! The Lakers led, 114–111.

But Smits responded with another jump hook. Once again, the Lakers gave the ball to Bryant.

The Pacers must not have believed his earlier basket, because they gave Bryant some room to shoot again. Once more he stutter-stepped, faked, stepped back, and . . .

Swish! Nothing but net again. Lakers 116, Pacers 113. "I just relaxed like I was in my backyard," Bryant said later.

The Pacers then answered with two free throws by Miller. But as the Pacer defense blanketed Bryant, Brian Shaw put back a miss by Rice to make the score 118–115. Then Smits hit two free throws to bring the Pacers back to within one at 118–117.

The Lakers had the ball with 28 seconds left. They tried to work down the clock. Forced to act before the 24-second clock ran out, Brian Shaw put up a shot.

It bounced off the rim.

Out of nowhere, Bryant flashed in, grabbed the rebound, and put it back to give the Lakers a 120–117 lead. The Pacers managed to sink a free throw in the final seconds, but Bryant and the Lakers came out on top, 120–118.

After the game, everyone wanted to talk about Kobe Bryant. "Kobe smelled it at the end of the game," said Coach Jackson, "and he lifted us."

"That was big-time tonight," added Glen Rice.

"He stepped up like a veteran. That just goes to show how much he's matured." A reporter then asked Shaq what Bryant had said when he had approached him after he'd fouled out in overtime. The big center smiled. "He said, 'Don't worry about it, I got it.'" That he certainly did. "That's what a one-two punch can do for you," he added. "When you injure your left hand, the right will step up and knock out the opponent."

Bryant even impressed Pacer coach Larry Bird, who had been one of the greatest clutch players in NBA history during his career with the Boston Celtics. "It was awesome," said Bird of Bryant's performance. "Every shot was all net," he said of Bryant's 28 points on 14 of 27 shooting from the field. "We knew Kobe was going to take over. It's just that we couldn't stop him."

Down three games to one, the Pacers didn't fold, winning game five in a rout, 120–87. But in game six, the Lakers wouldn't be denied. Behind O'Neal and Bryant, they won, 116–111, to capture the NBA championship.

Bryant scored 26 points in the finale, including

four critical free throws in the final 13 seconds. At the final buzzer, he and O'Neal embraced. The victory answered forever the question of whether the two stars could learn to play together.

That's bad news for the rest of the NBA, because Kobe Bryant, still one of the youngest players in the league, has *a lot* of basketball left to play.

Matt Christopher

Kobe Bryant	*Tara Lipinski*
Terrell Davis	*Mark McGwire*
Julie Foudy	*Greg Maddux*
Jeff Gordon	*Hakeem Olajuwon*
Wayne Gretzky	*Alex Rodriguez*
Ken Griffey Jr.	*Briana Scurry*
Mia Hamm	*Sammy Sosa*
Tony Hawk	*Venus and Serena Williams*
Grant Hill	
Derek Jeter	*Tiger Woods*
Randy Johnson	*Steve Young*
Michael Jordan	

The #1 Sports Series for Kids

MATT CHRISTOPHER

Read them all!

All available in paperback from Little, Brown and Company